MW01115361

Adult Coloring Book

30 Inspirational Quotes

Stress Relief With Positivity

To: _____

From: _____

My world is better with you in it

Palette Test Sheet

Thank You!

We want to thank you for purchasing this book!
If you enjoyed this book, then I'd like to ask you for a favor,
would you be kind enough to leave a review for this book
on Amazon? It'd be greatly appreciated!

Make sure you follow us:
facebook.com/unibulpress/
instagram.com/unibulpress/
pinterest.com/unibulpress/

unibulpress.com

If you have colored a page from our book and upload it
to any social media please make sure you tag us or link to
the book.

Thank you again for purchasing!

Made in the USA
Las Vegas, NV
10 October 2023

78856431R00037